QUIT SMOKING! WHILE SMOKING!

BY JOSEPH CROSS

SCRIPTOR HOUSE
THE EPITOME OF GREATNESS

Do You Want to Quit Smoking?
We Can Help!

Scriptor House LLC

2810 N Church St Wilmington, Delaware, 19802

www.scriptorhouse.com

Phone: +1302-205-2043

Published by Scriptor House LLC

Paperback ISBN: 979-8-88692-186-1

eBook ISBN: 979-8-88692-187-8

No cancerous vapors/e-cigarettes

No pills or gum

No patches

No acupuncture

No medications

No hypnosis

No gimmicks whatsoever

We all thought that vaping and e-cigarettes were the saving graces or the answer for all smokers. But now there's findings of the deadly dangers that they have caused people. This method is all we have with no side effects. Don't knock it till you've tried it.

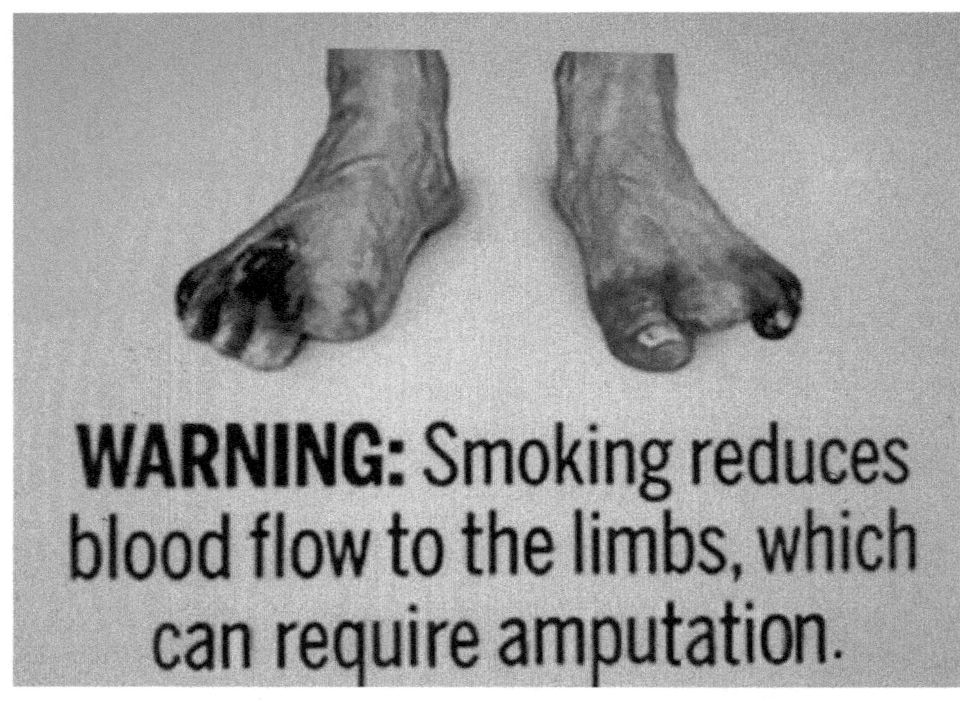

WARNING: Smoking reduces blood flow to the limbs, which can require amputation.

There are only two things that you must have, and that without it, this will not work for you. And that is THE **_WILL_** AND THE **_DETERMINATION_** TO STOP SMOKING. (Needless to say, if you don't want to stop smoking, don't worry, you won't.) You have to **_WANT_** to stop smoking, or you will **_NEVER_** stop smoking.

You can't do it for anyone else; you **must** do it for **yourself**.

I, the founder of this method, actually smoked for twenty-six years, a pack and a half a day. I tried several methods over and over, spent a lot of money to stop smoking, and never did. They won't tell you it's your **will** and **determination**, not the products that you stop smoking. It was only when I tried this method did I stop for good. And it's been twenty-six years since I've smoked a cigarette, and if **I** can do it, so can **you**.

I promise you don't need anything else to stop. This method you only have to buy it **_ONE TIME,_** not like the others, where you have to keep buying their products over and over until you stop or just get tired of spending your money and still smoking.

SO PAY YOUR <u>ONE</u>-TIME ONLY INVESTMENT OF $8.99 FOR THE ONLINE METHOD, AND YOU WON'T HAVE TO SEND ANOTHER DIME, AND YOUR SMOKING DAYS ARE OVER.

My name is Joseph Cross, and as I said before, I, too, was a heavy smoker at one time in my life. I used to smoke anywhere from one to a pack and a half a day, and I did that for thirty years. Having been born with bronchitis, it was difficult to breathe at times, and by me coughing up brown phlegm all the time, I wanted to stop smoking. I tried numerous ways to stop smoking, and none of them worked for me. I tried the patches, gum, etc. I know people who have been hypnotized and had acupuncture and still went back to smoking. Even after buying these products over and over, trying these methods that say you can cut down smoking until you stop completely never really knowing when that will be. Just waiting and hoping for the last time you have to buy any more of these products or just stop buying them because they're not working after spending wasted amounts of money. And what about the side effects that some of them have: headaches, nausea, rash, and to top it off, becoming suicidal. I was literally killing myself and didn't worry about that at all, as all smokers do. It had become an addiction that I couldn't shake. Once I had seen the effect it was having on me, with bronchitis and all, it was too late. **It's like being addicted to drugs, but it's legal.** Us smokers know how we got hooked on such a horrible habit, right? What is never mentioned is that no matter what you take or do while you are smoking to help you stop will never work unless you have the **will** and **determination** to stop. It is not the pill, gum, or anything else that makes you stop; it's the **will** and **determination** with some effort and a natural method to make it happen. So let's get to the most effective way ever to quit this horrible habit ***for good***.

We're going to get mind-set first.

ADMITTING that we have an addiction we **don't want** anymore. That's right! It will *never* work if we don't ***admit*** we really want to stop. Really look at the damage that it is doing to us, something that us smokers hardly ever do. We have to stop ignoring the inevitable fact that smoking **kills**. ***Admitting*** that we **don't want to smoke** anymore is the **first and most important** part of this process. We must finally realize and feel it in your gut that you **don't want this addiction anymore**. Remember, **IF YOU DON'T WANT TO STOP SMOKING, don't worry, YOU WON'T**.

The next step is realizing that it's **INSANE** to keep smoking when **you really want to stop**. The horrible smell it leaves in your mouth, clothes, and everything else, not to mention the physical effects and damage it causes to our body, ignoring all the commercials and advertising we see, read, and hear about the harm it causes, just like any other bad habit that we happen to obtain, whether it's overeating, gambling, drugs, alcohol, etc. It is important that we come to realize the ***insanity*** of continuing to keep doing something that we ***know*** is harmful to our **body, mind, and spirit**. But there's an upside to this insanity.

<u>**Believing**</u> that <u>**you**</u> <u>***can and will***</u> stop smoking.

Last but not least, putting **that** belief in the <u>**right method**</u> to use, without any e-cigarettes, chemicals, or medications, without any gum or patches that are supposed to work, and for some reason or another, they don't. Some people might have thought that it worked for them but only if they think about it, it was the **will and determination,** not the things they were taking. So even if you gave up on trying those methods, here's a method that can help you <u>***stop for good***</u>. You tried everything else, so why not try this natural way with no side effects. Also remember that you don't want to start another bad habit by overeating, as most of us do. Breath mints or gum helps to keep from eating too much. Some people might say that chewing gum is not good, but what's worse, gum or overeating? And you might want to add a little <u>***exercise***</u> to your routine, which is a <u>***good habit***</u>. And it also makes you feel good about yourself as well. You really have to put your total effort into this method, if you want it to work. This method has been kitchen tested, with myself and others with a 100 percent result. <u>Concentrate on this</u>: <u>**to get something you never had, you have to do something you've never done.**</u> And yes, I don't want you to stop smoking right now all at once. That's never gonna work. You have to cut down and build resistance all in one, week by week, month by month, until you're done. No more cigarettes with the confidence it's for good.

So let's get started.

SMOKING KILLS
STOP SMOKING
Lorem ipsum dolor sit amet, consectetuer adipiscing elit, sed diam nonummy nibh euismod tincidunt ut laoreet dolore magna aliquam erat volutpat. Ut wisi enim ad minim veniam, quis nostrud exerci tation ullamcorper suscipit lobortis nisl ut aliquip ex ea commodo consequat. Duis autem vel eum iriure dolor in hendrerit in vulputate velit esse molestie consequat.

THE QUIT SMOKING WHILE SMOKING METHOD

First things first, the **WILL** and **DETERMINATION** to stop smoking once and for all. As we mentioned earlier, without these two main factors, there's no use to even start this process. ***Second***, **count** the cigarettes you smoke in one day. That's right, how can you cut down on something if you don't know the average amount to **cut down** from. So yes, count how many cigarettes on an average you smoke in a day. What this is for is to start the procedure of **cutting down** the amount of cigarette you smoke daily. ***The third step*** is to start **building resistance** by waiting five to ten minutes before you smoke a cigarette, any and every time you get the urge. That's right, from the time when you **first get up in the morning until the time you go to bed at night**. And I mean ***every time*** you get the urge—from the time when your feet first hit the floor in the morning, after drinking coffee, after eating, or anything else that gives you the urge to smoke. This way, by waiting the five to ten minutes ***every time*** you have an urge to smoke, you are automatically **building resistance** while starting the process of **cutting down** on how many you smoke per day.

Building resistance is the ***most important*** part of this process as you will see when you start to progress using this method. So don't take it lightly. Please wait. It's only a few minutes.

Now, **DO THIS FOR A WEEK**, or two (depending on how fast you want to stop): **REMEMBER, do not smoke no more than the number of cigarettes you counted on that first day, and wait five to ten minutes whenever you get an urge or craving to smoke. It would also be good to keep track of this, writing down the amounts of cigarettes you're smoking and the minutes you're waiting each week. One more important thing is remembering not to start another bad habit when trying to stop one. In other words, do not start overeating, like most people do. Watch your eating habits. Breath mints, peppermint balls, or gum helps you from eating too much. Oh yeah, exercise!**

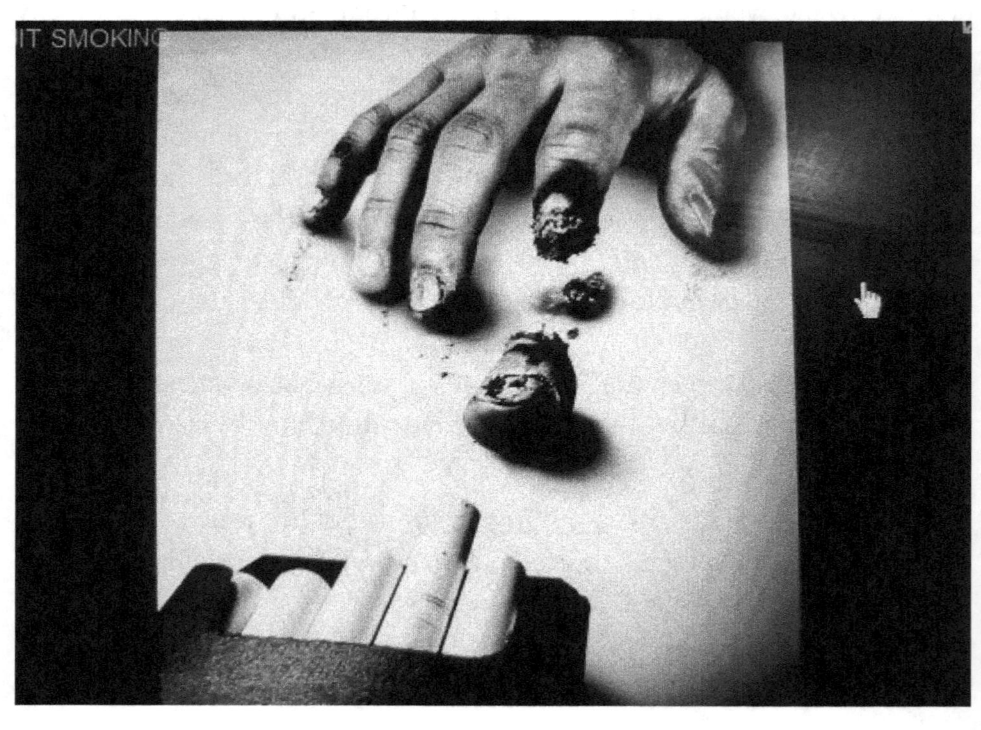
IT SMOKING

YOUR SMOKE-FREE LIFE

Over time, you will greatly lower your risk of death from lung cancer and other diseases.

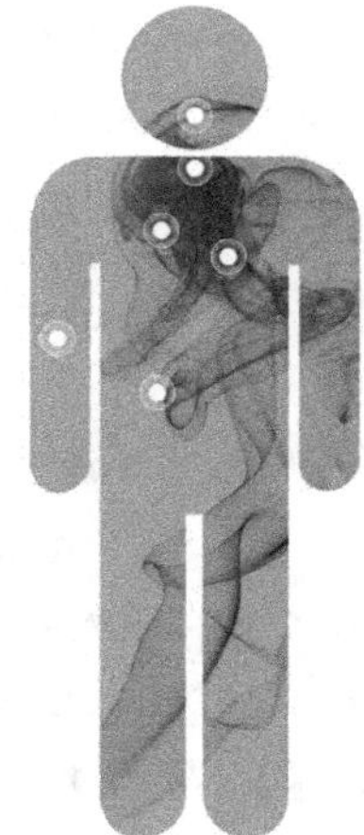

Within 20 minutes, your heart rate and blood pressure drop

Within 12 hours, the carbon monoxide level in your bloodstream drops to normal

Within 3 months, your circulation and lung function improves

After 9 months, you will cough less and breathe easier

After 1 year, your risk of coronary heart disease is cut in half

After 5 years, your risk of cancer of the mouth, throat, esophagus and bladder are cut in half

After 10 years, you are half as likely to die from lung cancer, and your risk of larynx or pancreatic cancer decreases

After 15 years, your risk of coronary heart disease is the same as a non-smoker's risk

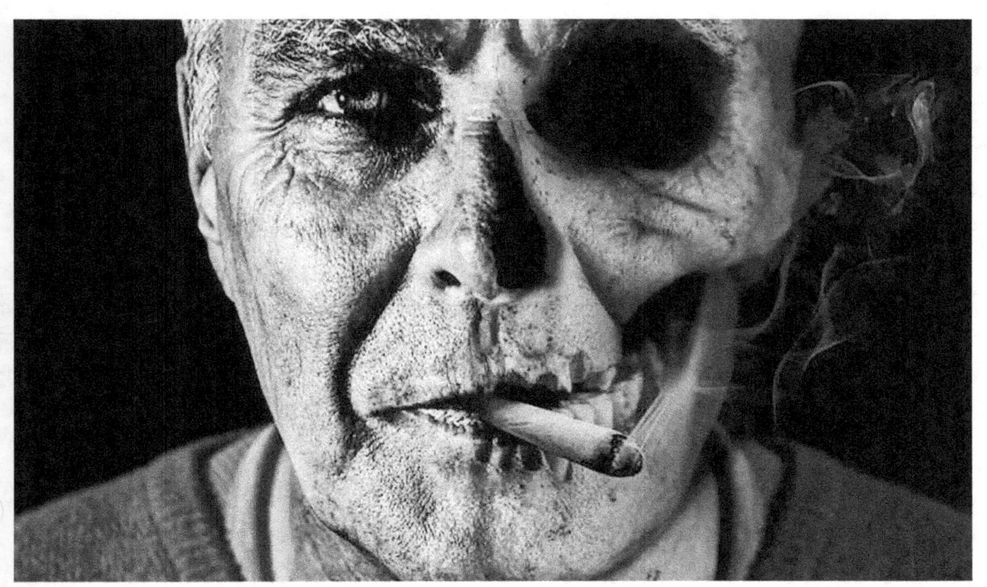

Now how do you feel? Do you feel like a little progress has been made? WHY, OF COURSE, IT HAS! And remember, ***to get something you never had, you have to do something you've never done.***

You may not have cut down yet, but you have built a little resistance between urges. Now here's where the cutting down comes in. A week or two has gone by.

Drop two cigarettes down from what you were smoking for the past week or two. For example, if you were smoking twenty a day, now you're going to only smoke eighteen a day. **And repeat step 1, 2, and 3**, but this time, when following the third step, I want you to wait ten to fifteen minutes. Yes, that's right, wait ten to fifteen **_minutes_** before each urge or craving you get to smoke. Keep in mind that the **longer** you wait, the **stronger** your resistance will become. **You can do it**. You just did it for five to ten minutes the past week or two. Now just count it as **just adding ten more minutes** than what you've just finished doing for the last week or so.

Now **_REMEMBER_, do not smoke any more than the number you are on from dropping the two cigarettes, and wait the full ten to fifteen minutes after each urge or craving for a cigarette. Also, take peppermint balls, breath mints, or gum instead of food. And of course, exercise!**

Can you see where we're going with this? While decreasing the amount of cigarettes you smoke, it takes care of cutting down to where you won't even notice. The same as you would do if you had the patch, gum, etc. But you're not spending extra money for those items or procedures. And waiting before each time you get the urge helps you build the resistance you will need, minute by minute, hour by hour, for when you stop for good.

It's been two to four weeks, and we're down to smoking two cigarettes less than you've smoked before, and waiting ten to fifteen minutes before each craving. Again, ***to get something you never had, you have to do something you've never done.***

Now let's drop two more cigarettes. You are now down to sixteen cigarettes a day if you started with twenty. Repeat steps 1, 2, and 3, but when you get to the third step, you're going to wait twenty *to thirty minutes* when you get a craving or urge to smoke.

Remember, **it's just ten minutes more than what you just finished waiting** for the last week or two. *And remember, peppermints or gum will take the place of putting food in your mouth. And exercise.*

At this point, it's very important that you *recognize how much you are accomplishing*. And I know that the waiting period is not easy, but you are doing it *because you really want this to work* and it **will** if you stay on course to the end. **Please do not take what you are accomplishing with a minimum of concern.** You are embarking on something **GREAT**, *and when finished, never having to do it again.* Just think of all the ways you've tried to stop: patches, pills, cold turkey, the whole nine yards. **And now even just up to this point, you can see that it's going to work this time.**

What are you smoking?

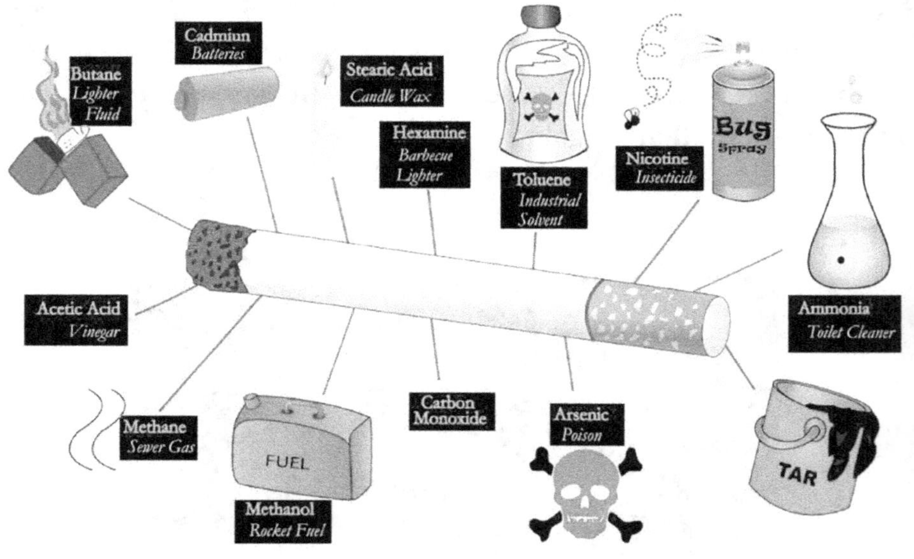

Guess what! It's been three to six weeks, and you are doing just fine. And I think you know the drill by now.

That's right, let's drop two more cigarettes, and whatever number you've started with, you are now smoking six cigarettes less. *Now that's a great accomplishment*. Remember, *to get something you never had, you have to do something you've never done.*

Repeat steps 1, 2, and 3, and you now going to *wait thirty to forty-five minutes, a whole half hour plus, after each urge or craving when you get to step 3, and remember, peppermints or gum will take the place of putting food in your month. <u>Overeating is a bad habit too.</u>* So exercise.

Okay, now, it's been a month or two, and you know that anything you do for thirty days or more becomes a habit, but this is a good one. So here it is, four to eight weeks has gone by, and you're going to drop two more cigarettes, which bring it down to eight less than you started with. **Repeat steps 1, 2, and 3**. When at step 3, you're going to wait forty-five to sixty minutes. Yes! A whole hour if you dare, which should not be that much of a problem, right! Now I am pretty sure you know exactly how this is going to play out. **Every week, or two**, you are going to **drop two cigarettes** and **add ten to fifteen more minutes waiting time** between urges or cravings. Also, remember, the longer you wait after each craving, the stronger your resistance will be. **You are going to do this until you are down to two cigarettes a day**. That's right, which will take another month or so, meaning the whole process should take about four to six months, or less. While waiting that length of time, several hours between urges or cravings. And then, do that for a week, or two, with just smoking two cigarettes a day, for a week or two, and guess what, <u>**YOU'RE DONE!**</u>

Your resistance should be so strong now that even when you get the urge to smoke, **you won't, because this is the end of this nasty addition forever. Always remember, if you don't pick it up, you won't smoke it. It's just that simple.**

You have built a resistance so strong and have not smoked when you really wanted to for quite some time now, so that's what you use from now on. **<u>Building the resistance you have now means you don't have to smoke even when you really want to.</u>** And don't let your head tell you any different.

Do not let your mind or thoughts trick you into thinking that you can have just one cigarette and it'll be all right. ONE IS TOO MANY, AND A PACK IS NEVER ENOUGH. And always remember, <u>TO GET SOMETHING YOU NEVER HAD, YOU HAVE TO DO SOMETHING YOU'VE NEVER DONE</u>. <u>STAY STOPPED!</u>

Also, the peppermint balls, breath mints, or gum will keep up from overeating. Use these items to keep from eating too much. I'm twenty-six years off cigarettes and still get the urge to smoke, but I know if I do, all this work and time that I haven't smoke will be in vain, and I don't want that, and I won't let my mind trick me ever again into smoking again. Use these items to keep from eating too much. Oh yeah, exercise!

<u>WINNERS NEVER QUIT, AND QUITTERS NEVER WIN.</u>

CIGARETTE COMPOUND
TAR
ARSENIC
LEAD
FORMALDEHYDE
MERCURY
POLONIUM-210
CARBON MONOXIDE
NICOTINE

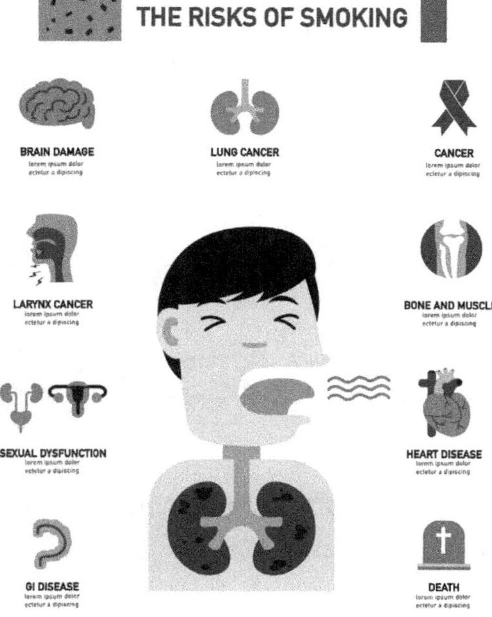

THE RISKS OF SMOKING
BRAIN DAMAGE
lorem ipsum dolor
ectetur a dipiscing
LUNG CANCER
lorem ipsum dolor
ectetur a dipiscing
CANCER
lorem ipsum dolor
ectetur a dipiscing
LARYNX CANCER
lorem ipsum dolor
ectetur a dipiscing
BONE AND MUSCLE
lorem ipsum dolor
ectetur a dipiscing
SEXUAL DYSFUNCTION
lorem ipsum dolor
ectetur a dipiscing
HEART DISEASE
lorem ipsum dolor
ectetur a dipiscing
GI DISEASE
lorem ipsum dolor
ectetur a dipiscing
DEATH
lorem ipsum dolor
ectetur a dipiscing

WITHIN 20 MINUTES OF QUITTING SMOKING...
YOUR BODY BEGINS A SERIES OF CHANGES THAT CONTINUE FOR YEARS.
20 MINUTES
YOUR HEART RATE DROPS.
2 - 3
YOUR HEART ATTACK RISK BEGINS TO DROP. YOUR LUNG FUNCTION BEGINS TO IMPROVE.
1 YEAR
YOUR ADDED RISK OF CORONARY HEART DISEASE IS HALF THAT OF A SMOKER'S
10 YEARS
YOUR LUNG CANCER DEATH RATE IS ABOUT HALF THAT OF A SMOKER'S. YOUR RISK OF CANCERS OF THE MOUTH, THROAT, ESOPHAGUS, BLADDER, KIDNEY AND PANCREAS DECREASES
12 HOURS
CARBON MONOXIDE LEVEL IN YOUR BLOOD DROPS TO NORMAL.
1-9 MONTHS
YOUR COUGHING AND SHORTNESS OF BREATH DECREASE.
5 YEARS
YOUR STROKE RISK IS REDUCED TO THAT OF A NONSMOKER'S 5 TO 15 YEARS AFTER QUITTING
15 YEARS
YOUR RISK OF CORONARY HEART DISEASE IS BACK TO THAT OF A NONSMOKER'S
FOR MORE INFORMATION VISIT CDC.GOV

I just want to say thanks to the people that help make this method a success:

Scott Simmons

Sandi Kent

Yusuf Cross

Renee Rogers

And last but not least, thank you for trying this method, and God bless you all.

No Smoking

About the Author

Joseph Cross is a singer/entertainer who was born with bronchitis, smoked for about twenty-six years. The more he smoked, the more the phlegm built up in his throat to the point it was hard to sing because of coughing so much from the phlegm that built. So he used this method to stop smoking, and it's been twenty-six years since he had a cigarette, and the real good part about it is that there is no more phlegm in his throat and he's still singing in Las Vegas, the entertainment capital of world, he might add.

In addition, please go online and check out the single, father and son song, sang by Joseph and Yusuf Cross titled "Winner's n Quitter's, go to; josephcross.hearnow.com it's with iTunes and Amazon, once again thank you for your support God Bless.